It Shouldn't Hurt to *Smile*

Devin LuRenz

This page intentionally left blank.

Copyright ©2021 Devin LuRenz

Copyright © 2021 by Devin LuRenz, First Edition.

All rights reserved. No part of this publication may be reproduced, distributed, or transmitted in any form or by any means, including photocopying, recording, or other electronic or mechanical methods, without the prior written permission of the publisher, except in the case of brief quotations embodied in critical reviews and certain other noncommercial uses permitted by copyright law. For permission requests, email the publisher @devinlurenz@gmail.com.

Quantity sales. Special discounts are available on quantity purchases by corporations, associations, and others. For details, email the publisher @devinlurenz@gmail.com.

Printed in the United States of America.

ISBN 979-8-7459405-3-8

Cover Design By Preston Foster, Influent Creations

DEDICATION

This book of poetry and every good thing I attempt to accomplish, is dedicated to the person who always believed in me, even when I didn't believe in myself. Thanks Mom, you are missed beyond measure.

Annie G. Cropper, Sunrise: 4/30/1940 – Sunset: 3/1/2018

Copyright ©2021 Devin LuRenz

Life Happens; Sometimes, it hurts.

Copyright ©2021 Devin LuRenz

HI MOM

If I had one wish,
That I knew would come true.
I'd wish you were here,
So, I could hug you.

Tell you the things,
I never got to say.
Cling to you tightly,
So, you couldn't get away.

I know this can't happen,
I've accepted that now.
In my heart, you're still here,
And you'll always be around.

Copyright ©2021 Devin LuRenz

ACKNOWLEDGMENTS

To the open-minded and self-accepting men and women who came before me and to all of those who believe that a person's thoughts and individual ideas should not be hidden, stifled or otherwise dismissed, I thank you.

To my husband, George and kids, Scooter and Doodle who have always supported my writing, whether they totally understood it or not, thanks for listening, accepting and believing in my abilities. Love you all!

To my mom, Annie G. my biggest fan, my forever believer, my most supreme admirer, thank you. Thank you for loving me when I didn't love myself and for convincing me that I was worthy. Thank you for being my safety net when I didn't know I needed one. Thank you for going above and beyond to ensure I had access to all the things that were not available to you and for making the seemingly impossible things, possible. You were taken from us far too soon but will live on forever in our hearts and minds.

To ALL my sisters, related by blood and those that I've adopted along the way, I thank you. For whether you're aware or not, you have each played a significant role in my personal transformation. I actually like me, now…I haven't always. Faye, Debbie, Phoebe, Bessie, Zina, Tonya, Don & KJ, I could not love and respect you more if we had grown up in the same house. I would gladly share mirror space with all of you!

I thank God for the gift of writing and the courage to finally use it. I am excitedly becoming the woman I was created to be, and it feels AMAZING! I hope I do you proud.

Copyright ©2021 Devin LuRenz

This page intentionally left blank.

Copyright ©2021 Devin LuRenz

We must accept that some things are beyond our control.

CALLED HOME

You may not see me near you,
But know that I'm not far away.
When you speak to me, I hear you.
We'll speak face to face again one day.

I'm sorry for leaving you so soon,
Trust me, the choice was not mine.
He who sits upon the throne,
Told me that it was my time.

It's not the pain that hurts;
It's the loss.

WHEN I LOST YOU

Love,

Hurt

and

Pain,

Never existed in the

Same place before.

Then, I lost you.

Now, those words

Have new meaning.

"Your eyes reveal the pain that exists in your heart."

HEART'S RAIN

Outside,

The Sun

Shines brightly.

Inside

My heart,

It still rains.

STREAKS OF PAIN

Saltwater stings.
My eyes pause
Before opening
To allow the free flow
Of salt streams.

I smile
through the tears
And pray
that joy will come
In the morning.

RAINDROPS OF PEACE

Raindrops delicately falling

Synchronized sounds of nature

Awaken the senses and soothe

The rumblings of discord

in the world around us

Momentarily

restoring

serenity

and

peace.

THOUGHTS AFIRE

My mind
Runs away with me
Playing hateful games
Flashing images
Of that
Which no longer exists.

Again,
I fall to my knees
And weep.
Allowing the emptiness
Of an insurmountable loss
To be expressed through my tears.

BETTER DAYS

Saddened

By gray suns.

Illuminated

By hope.

But,

too afraid

to dream

Of better days.

DARK CLOUDS

Dark clouds in the distance,
Moving closer to where I stand.
Afraid of what's coming,
I reach out for your hand.

The space near me is now empty,
I feel nothing but the air.
I thought you stood beside me,
But you're no longer there.

Enlightenment.

You were not created to bear the brunt of everyone's burdens.

LIFE WITH PEOPLE

Life is filled with people,

Who come and go as needed.

Some of them are see through,

The presence of others is fleeted.

People you need stay put,

They're in your life for the duration.

Treat them well so that they know,

Life would not be the same without them.

To speak callously, without thinking, reveals one's true thoughts.

WORDS HURT

Hurtful

Words

Cause

Scars

Not

Visible

To the naked eye.

MEAN PEOPLE

People

May taunt and tease

Or

Just be mean to you.

Know that their own

Insecurities

May be what

They're clinging to.

MY HEART BROKE UP WITH ME

I promised my heart

That I would not

Give it away freely again.

That I would protect it

From being hurt

By those that did not value it.

My heart broke up with me

Because,

I did not keep my promise.

You are not defined by another's opinion of you; Only your own.

FORGIVE, DON'T FORGET

Forgive what they did

To make you question

Your worth.

Don't forget

How you felt

When

You realized

That they

Were wrong.

A heart is like a glass; Only as strong as the hand that holds it.

DESTINY AND PATIENCE

Sometimes,
Things aren't meant to be,
No matter how hard we try.
Just be patient,
And your destiny
Will reveal
What you need,
And why.

Empowerment.

FLAWED PERFECTION

The day I walked away from me,
I was angry and confused.
How dare someone lay claim to me,
And leave me feeling used.

I should have yelled; I should have screamed.
I should have stood up for myself.
Was the issue as serious as it seemed,
To make me yield to someone else?

Too afraid of judgment, to stand up and be heard.
Scared of what may be said about me,
So, I did not utter a single word.
I could hear it all, but I could not see.

When I finally opened my eyes
And accepted who I was,
It was then that I realized,
I was perfect, in spite of my flaws.

PERFECT IN HIS EYES

I've been told that I had big lips.

That my legs were small.

That I had no hips,

And that I was too tall.

They'd say my skin was too brown.

I failed the paper bag test.

My nose was too round,

And I had a flat chest.

At first, I believed it all,

Until I finally realized

Others' opinions of me, don't matter at all,

Because I'm perfect in God's eyes.

SHATTERED CAGE

Captured, but not dismayed,

I am still hopeful though, temporarily caged.

The sun still shines and gently bathes my face.

My future will not be determined by the obstacles in place.

What I was born accomplish, has not changed one single bit.

My mission is clear, and I willingly accept it.

A temporary setback only strengthens my resolve,

Intensifies my focus and quantifies my cause.

I am not intended to be shackled nor constrained another day.

The cage door has been shattered, so that I may fly away.

JOURNEY TO SELF-ACCEPTANCE

My own reflection once bothered me,

I didn't see who I wanted to be.

Plagued by opinions of society,

Convinced to be brown made me unworthy.

Consumed by feelings of inadequacy,

Hoping one day to be accepted by me.

Much time passed and gradually,

I learned to look inside of me.

Soon, I realized that it was my opinion of me,

That would define my ultimate destiny.

To become the very best version of me.

I now love and accept the reflection I see.

And there is no one else, I would rather be.

NO MORE GRAY SKIES

Blue skies can seem gray,

On the brightest of days.

When all hope has faded away,

And left dread in its place.

Look up and be reminded,

That you're where you need to be.

The mountain was high, but you climbed it,

So, continue to believe.

Don't slow down, you must press on,

For the paths remaining are not few.

Let each experience be a lesson,

You will use to see you through.

When you see the finish line,

Run faster, forget the brakes.

Always keep faith front of mind,

And don't quit, you've got what it takes.

BELIEVE

Dreams

Do come true,

As long as you believe.

Forces

Will work through you,

To realize what's conceived.

You never know how weak you are, until presented with what once made you weak. You are strong enough to overcome any momentary weakness.

THE WEAKENED

Weakened last weekend.

But not weak this week.

More blessed than stressed,

And more assertive than meek.

Pray more to say more,

And hear more in return.

Open mind, open heart,

Yet, so much more to learn.

It's not the time I'm awake that scares me; It's the time that my eyes are open.

VOICES IN MY HEAD

Quiet all around, but not in my head,
The voices just will not be silent.
Day after day, waking with dread,
Hoping today will be less violent.

Working hard to focus on the tasks at hand,
And ignore the voices only I can hear.
Closing my eyes as tightly as I can,
Wanting inner thoughts to be happy and clear.

Another long day has come to an end,
The voices are finally at rest.
Tomorrow is a new day, I will try again,
And know that I am strong enough to pass any test.

Inner strength often evolves from external entanglements.

Encouragement.

FLAWED, BUT FAVORED

They said you wouldn't make it,
That you weren't worth your salt.
For years you had to take it,
Bear things that weren't your fault.

Through it all, you persevered,
Because you knew you would.
You're flawed, but highly favored,
And all things work together for your good.

EASY DREAMS

What

You can accomplish

Is

Far beyond your dreams.

What

You once thought was impossible,

Is

Easier than it seems.

When new obstacles seem to appear as soon as you've surpassed another; Success may be closer than you think. Keep going.

EASY DREAMS

Success

Can be yours

If

You only believe.

Focus

and

Visualize,

And

Your dreams

Will be achieved.

Success is the culmination of hard work, faith and belief in one's ability to overcome obstacles;

Real or Imagined.

DON'T STOP TO BREATHE

Inhale.

Exhale.

Accept.

You're still here.

You continue to exist.

All is **not** lost,

When you fail

All is lost,

When you give up.

BE TRUE TO YOU

Celebrate your accomplishments,
No matter how small.
It's OK if others don't celebrate,
Or compliment you at all.

Do as you were meant to do,
Don't mind what others say.
Those same people may come to you,
And wish you well one day.

No matter if they come or not,
Always look forward, never back.
Some people want what you've got.
But they'll never admit that.

The life you live, should be your own,
You live for no one else.
You were born into this world alone,
So, always be true to thine own self.

JUST BELIEVE

Eyes wide open,

But I still could not see.

I had lost all hope,

Darkness surrounded me.

Wanted to try,

But, too scared to fail.

I started to cry,

And let fear prevail.

Then a voice spoke to me,

Told me not to fear.

I just needed to believe,

And my way would be made clear.

Darkness went away,

As did all nervousness.

It was a brand-new day,

And today, I was fearless.

BE GREAT

Let no one tell you,

That you're not enough.

You are.

Let no one tell you,

That you do not matter.

You do.

Let no one make you cry,

For they do not deserve your tears.

Let no one force you,

To question your existence.

You are meant to be here.

You are meant to flourish.

You are meant to do more than exist

You are meant to be great.

So, do that

Be great

Today

Tomorrow

Forever.

Don't be angry because others appear to be leaving you behind. Be motivated to do more and create your own successes. There is no limit to what you can do.

NO LONGER AFRAID

I was afraid.

I tried to move forward,

Stand up and be counted.

I fell down.

I got up.

Still afraid.

Tried to move forward,

I fell down, again.

I looked up,

Got up, again.

Determined, faith-filled and confident.

They tried to push me, again.

But this time,

I did not fall.

I am no longer afraid.

FEAR AS FIRE

It's ok to be afraid.

Let fear

Fuel the

Emotional fire

That burns

Within you.

LIFE BLOOMS

Love-starved, smile deprived,
Not quite sure how I survived.
Head hung low; confidence gone,
Nowhere to go, felt so alone.

Then one day, I lifted my head,
Hope had returned, gone was the dread.
What I needed most, had finally found me,
Life started over and bloomed all around me.

BECOMING A BUTTERFLY

Never really popular,

Or good at being seen.

I guess I was the little girl,

Who fell somewhere in between.

Didn't really like attention,

Way to bashful, much too shy.

Taunted, teased, bullied and then some,

Never imagined I would be a butterfly.

To those who can relate,

But don't quite know why.

You're afraid to participate,

And let opportunities pass you by.

Know that you are beautiful,

Love the reflection you see.

Accept it and be grateful,

And become who you were born to be.

Accepting the truth allows tangled emotions to untangle themselves.

IT SHOULDN'T HURT TO SMILE

You get knocked down at every turn,

Why should you continue?

There are many lessons left to learn,

And what you need to succeed is within you.

The pain you feel will start to fade,

With each step and every mile.

Give thanks and celebrate the progress you've made,

It shouldn't hurt to smile.

IT'S MY TIME

To find me.

To know me.

To love me.

To choose me.

To embrace me.

To ignore the naysayers,

Who will never be me.

My journey has not been easy,

But it did not defeat me.

It's finally my time to be,

Unapologetically ME.

love

The(re) Is No *End* to Transformation.

"Once you've got it trigulated, nothing and nobody can ever stop you. You got this, dollbaby."

~My Favorite Lady, Annie G."

Made in the USA
Middletown, DE
15 June 2023